Cryptocurrency

Realizing The Potential Of The Market For Digital Currencies A Comprehensive Guide To Trading Cryptocurrency Confidently

(Investing In Cryptocurrency Assets)

Haywood Mendoza

TABLE OF CONTENT

Price Action Confluence 1
Investing in Cryptocurrencies 20
The workings of cryptocurrencies 37
Cryptocurrency Trading and Investment 79
How is blockchain technology being used by businesses? 105
Using Ethereum for programming 134
Issues with Ethereum You May Experience . 136

Price Action Confluence

Confluence may be used to create a customized investing plan when Price Action is your primary trading method. We covered how to utilize price action to choose entry and exit points for your trading strategy in the last chapter. This chapter will examine the use of confluence in the development of trading strategies.

Keep a careful watch on trends as you would with any Price Action transaction. Confluence trade setups need a thorough examination of price fluctuations since Price Action relies on following price changes.

Confluence is often characterized as the interplay of two or more levels. Within a single currency pair, this exchange takes place. As a result, you must pay attention to the different levels of price activity. We will be focusing on three distinct levels for the duration of this book: support, resistance, and trend. You must monitor these three levels in order to identify confluence.

The technique works because of how the many layers interact with one another. Finding the intersection of levels allows you to pinpoint entry and departure positions as well as potential breakout signals.

Regarding Levels of Resistance and Support
Finding highs and lows is the quickest and easiest technique to identify support and resistance levels. Without using technical analysis tools, this is the most straightforward method of locating such levels. You may reasonably be certain that the support and resistance levels you select to use for technical analysis will turn out to be correct. The platform determines these levels by comparing the trend to the highs and lows of the period being studied.

You may identify your levels by marking three consecutive hits on the levels you have defined, much as we have described in other portions of this book. These successive strikes need to be within the range. You need to be pretty certain that any breakouts or breakthroughs fall inside the range you are monitoring. Watch out for points that break through a resistance level since this may indicate the onset of a new resistance level. Likewise, you should exercise caution if price movement breaks through a floor since this might indicate the appearance of a new floor. You might enter or quit at the incorrect point if you don't recognize this possibility.

An obvious sign of a new floor or ceiling is a "double top" or "double bottom." Two strikes over the resistance threshold you've determined constitute a double top. When there is a bullish trendline, this is shown. So you've determined a ceiling by identifying three consecutive hits. Once a hit is detected over the resistance threshold, the signal returns to the mean. You have just seen a double top if the subsequent hit breaks over the resistance level. You should now anticipate a breakthrough. The third hit will climb over the roof when the breakout happens. You may infer that the new ceiling is currently in place from this.

On the other hand, a double bottom is defined as price action that penetrates the floor twice in a row. A negative tendency may be detected in this. As a result, when the trendline strikes below the floor twice in a row, a new floor is formed. The third strike may therefore be anticipated to land below the floor. If you want to play off the rebound, this can be a terrific entrance point.

Confluence happens in this study when the general trendline crosses both the designated levels of support and resistance. Therefore, what you may anticipate going ahead will ultimately be determined by the trendline.

Recognizing the trend

Use your platform's charting feature to compute the trend line to make things easier. The support and resistance levels should then be determined using the data shown in the chart itself. As the currency pair trades within its range, pay close attention to the engulfing candlesticks as they might indicate a change in trend.

At this stage, it's crucial to remember that even if the price movement is see-sawing, the trend line will finally decide whether it is a bullish or bearish trend. Charts that provide data for the last 24 to 48 hours should always be analyzed. However, you may examine larger time periods in order to find comparable trends.

For the purpose of identifying recurrent trends, some investors prefer to look at data going back a week. In these situations, it's possible that the time span you're looking at doesn't accurately represent the market trend. Despite the fact that this is fairly rare, it's conceivable that you are seeing a time that is notable for its unique trade activity.

It should be mentioned that in the case of FOREX, trends are quite transient. Unlike stockholders, FOREX traders practically live in the moment. Investors in stocks examine the 20, 50, and 200-day moving averages. These are unmistakable signs of potential changes in stock pricing. In the world of FOREX, anything may happen, particularly during uncertain times. You must thus concentrate on the most recent information.

Nevertheless, over longer timescales, a tendency is quite evident. Therefore, it is worthwhile to examine lengthier time periods in order to verify your hypotheses. Furthermore, if there are noteworthy occurrences occurring in your immediate environment, it could be worthwhile to pay greater attention to patterns that extend beyond the previous 48 hours. It's possible that price activity was moving one way but abruptly changed course due to unanticipated circumstances. Consider instances like terrorist attacks, massive corporate failures, or significant political events in this situation.

Confluence of Trendlines
When trendlines converge, you can be positioning yourself for a breakout or a breakthrough, which would both result in a strong decrease. Understanding the places at which you expect confluence may thus help you succeed or prevent failure.

We'll examine three instances of trendline confluence in this section.

Confluence of the following levels: Countertrend confluence, Support level confluence, and Resistance level confluence.

In each of these scenarios, the trendline is used as the primary tool for choosing the trade setting and ensuring that you enter or exit at the proper time. Let's examine these settings in more depth now.

Level Confluence of Support
In a setup like this, you are essentially betting on a breakthrough. Please remember that in order to establish your degree of support, you must identify at least three hits. Additionally, the price movement may or may not indicate a resistance level. Setting up a support and resistance level is not required. The sole need in this case is to define a precise support level. In fact, if you see large surges, you can be positioning yourself for a major profit.

The trendline must be situated below the support level you have mentioned. This is the crucial aspect. You have passed the deadline if the trend line is above the level of support. You may still be able to ride the wave to the top, but because you entered the trade after confluence—that is, the moment at which the trendline formally meets the support level—you can't expect to maximize your profit. You can be in for a big gain if you chance to enter just after confluence. However, the likelihood that you may miss the breakout increases the later you arrive.

Here are the requirements for setting up the trade:

First, clearly define at least three points that represent the strength of the support. If there are more, you can be certain that this is the lowest number. At this point, the price movement you are seeing has a very apparent support level.

Then, make sure that your trendline is increasing. This is significant since a flat or declining trendline is ineffective in this situation. You are in position for a substantial rise if you can spot the trendline that originates from a breakthrough.

After that, place your entrance point at the anticipated support level. You predict that the trendline will cross the support level at this location. This entry point may be automatically configured in your trade settings to make things easier. The deal will only be executed in this manner if the point is reached.

Last but not least, limit the size of your stop-loss to 20 pip maximum. This is significant in the event that the price, for whatever reason, falls below the support level. Set your take-profit point in accordance with the risk-to-reward ratio that you are using. For instance, you might set your risk to reward ratio to be 1:3 if you believe the benefit would be significant. Therefore, if your stop-loss is set at 20 pip, your take-profit might be set at 60 pip. Your transaction will become very successful as a result of this.

Don't initiate another trade if you quit a deal but the price continues to rise. No one can predict with certainty when the price will start to decline again. Therefore, it is advisable to wait for the price to return to normal. You can be observing a new support level if you discover that it doesn't affect the prior degree of support. Repeat the process once a double bottom confirms the potential existence of a new support level.

Confluence of Resistance
Similar to how the support level confluence trade is the reverse of this sort of trade. Avoiding being caught into a dropping price is the goal of this transaction. This might cause you to lose a significant amount of money in addition to zapping your earnings. Therefore, it's vital to be sure you have a solid understanding of what can occur.

The anticipation that a resistance level will change into a new support level is known as a resistance level confluence. When the price falls, this is conceivable. Although there are many causes behind this, you may take advantage of this tendency to profit when things are going well. You do not, however, believe that the price will rise over the support level.

Here, you can both generate money and keep from becoming wasted.

How to put up this transaction is as follows:

Find the price action's support level first by monitoring it. If there are many hits, you can very well be certain of this level. Keep a watch on this if there is a breakout followed by a return to the mean since it can point to a new support level.

Keep a watch on the first support level next, as this is likely to change into the next resistance level. This is because the price may not immediately return to its mean value. Instead, it will reach the support level before falling once again. The fact that the new resistance level has been reached is shown by this.

Look at the trendline after that. The trendline is likely to be moving horizontally (trading sideways) or exhibiting a very small upward or downward trend. You are receiving a misleading signal if there is a pronounced upward or negative trend since this might just be a sign of volatility.

Finally, adhere to the candlesticks. Look at the price action's lowest point before it begins to rise again. You may place your trade at the bottom and wait to make money on the rebound when the price movement bounces back up after hitting the new resistance level.

It's crucial to exercise caution with this trade because you risk entering it at what you thought was the support level just to discover that the price movement really broke through the floor. As a result, you risk taking a beating. Please keep in mind that this sort of transaction nearly typically indicates a horizontal trendline. Any other trendline will just serve as a false alarm.

Confluence of Countertrends
You are interacting with a declining trend in this arrangement. Determining the resistance level is thus crucial since it will show you where the biggest profit is likely to occur. Support levels are also not that important. To determine where the low points may occur, it would be helpful to look for any double or triple bottoms. You may use this to assist you in setting up your entrance point.

Because the trendline is trending lower, this setup is countertrend, but you are still hoping that the price will rise until it hits the bottom again. You should be aware that the platform will determine your support level. Making deals thus occurs when the distance between the trendline and support level is at its greatest. This will allow for a greater recovery. Less money is possible for you to make the closer the trendline is to the support level. You can also be on the verge of a turnabout. To avoid missing the reversal, it would be prudent to wait to act on this.

Look for any triple or double tops to set up the trade. This will enable you to pinpoint the areas where you may anticipate the resistance level to be. After that, have a look at the lows so you can use them as entry points. Finally, decide where to enter and leave the situation depending on the highs and lows you've determined.

If you want to execute many transactions in a single session, this method might be quite helpful. Although you may not see a lot of results, this tactic will undoubtedly help you establish yourself.

Stop evading the hunt

It is usually advised to use stop-loss orders in each transaction while trading FOREX. When you don't want to spend all of your time at your terminal, this is extremely crucial. Some investors prefer to put up their deals and then leave the platform to handle everything else. You must thus establish stop-loss levels on each and every transaction.

Simply place your stop-loss price below your entry point to do this. A 20 pip stop-loss threshold was already advised. If your entry point is 10, for example, you may place your stop-loss at 9.80.

The belief that the price will rise even if it has fallen below your entry point is the motivation for placing a stop-loss below your entry. Therefore, you may still profit from the price increase. You must cut your losses before they balloon if the price does not increase for whatever reason.

Now, every other investor has established their stop-loss point exactly as you have. It is safe to presume that almost all investors have their stop-loss points set up within an acceptable range. This implies that a deluge of stop-loss orders is triggered when the price abruptly drops. This causes the price to drop even further.

Some investors like looking for stop-loss orders to take advantage of prices that are below average. This is referred to as "stop hunting." You must be acutely aware of the various stop-loss points that other investors are putting up in order to profit from this kind of arrangement. Then, your goal is to profit from the stops so that you may purchase the currency pair at its cheapest position.

This transaction is very speculative. This suggests that there is no guarantee that the price will increase at the chosen entry point. As more and more stop-loss orders are placed, the price may really continue to decline. Then you can find yourself trapped in a situation where the price is rapidly decreasing. The rebound may not even return to the entering location at that point, thus nothing is certain.

Playing the countertrend technique is an excellent method to play the "stop hunting" game. Of course, a dropping trendline would be necessary (and the stop-loss orders should reflect that). If this is the case, there is a good likelihood that the price will bounce back at the support level for the particular currency pair.

For novices, stop hunting is not advised. This is why you should become acquainted with the several trend techniques we have described in this chapter first. After that, you can reasonably predict any price changes that could occur so that you can set up your trades appropriately. While stop hunting may undoubtedly result in large rewards, it's important to be vigilant for phony signals. When there is a large sell volume while the trendline is rising, these indications may flash. Therefore, keep a watch on trading volume since this is the greatest sign that several stop-loss orders will be activated at once.

Investing in Cryptocurrencies

Guidelines to remember and traps to avoid

This chapter is for you if the recent media coverage of cryptocurrencies has peaked your interest in the topic and you want to check out the market for yourself. Even if you don't already have a brokerage account, you'll discover that buying and selling cryptocurrencies is a really easy procedure.

The method

Choose the cryptocurrency in which you wish to invest. At CoinMarketCap or

CoinCap, you may see all the ones that are currently accessible, along with their price and market capitalization. At the moment, Bitcoin, Ethereum, and Ripple are the three most widely used cryptocurrencies.

Following your choice of cryptocurrency, you must decide on an exchange with which to work. A market platform where you may buy or sell publicly traded assets (shares/equities) is what an exchange essentially is. Cryptocurrencies have their own exchanges, which can be found at places like NASDAQ and NYSE, much like ordinary corporate stocks, which have them. Please be aware that not every cryptocurrency can be supported by an exchange. Additionally, some of them may not be available where you live. Therefore, thoroughly peruse the exchanges and choose one that appeals to you. The following criteria should be used to evaluate the exchange: public perception, supported payment methods, transaction fees, geographic restrictions, supported cryptocurrencies, and simplicity of use. The two exchanges with the most users are CoinBase and Kraken. Because CoinBase meets every need for me, I personally utilize it. And thus far, there haven't been any problems; the travel has been safe and easy. To join up and get a $10 bonus on your first trade, click the link below.

You will need to validate your identification (passport, driver's license, etc.) after choosing an appropriate exchange before you may register an account. You will be able to add/withdraw money and start trading as soon as the account is setup. You will be charged a very tiny fee for each transaction, just as on any other trading platform, in order to maintain the exchange.

You may be asking why your ID is needed because cryptocurrencies are meant to be decentralized and accommodating to users' choices for privacy and anonymity. Here's the problem, however. The cryptocurrency exchange requires initial payments in fiat currency to allocate you crypto-coins to trade with, even if the transactions themselves are secret. Additionally, there is a non-zero possibility of financial fraud wherever fiat money is used. Therefore, the exchange does need your personal details to confirm your fiat money in order to prevent problems with counterfeit fiat currency (stolen credit cards, etc.). Once your identity has been confirmed, you may trade privately on the site.

Precautions to take

Before making your investments, it pays to be aware of the apparent and not-so-obvious blunders given the current market volatility. Here are some things to remember to avoid becoming the next "riches to rags" tale.

The most important thing for you to be aware of is that there is no way to cancel or get a refund for a bitcoin transaction made via an exchange. Therefore, make sure everything is correct before you exchange your crypto-coins.

Invest only in cryptocurrencies with a solid track record and/or trustworthiness. You don't want someone to steal your money and flee. So conduct your research and only invest in ventures that you are confident in or that have a solid track record. Avoid cryptocurrencies that seem to be fraudulent and just have a nice website but no reliable staff or clear vision.

Avoid keeping an excessive amount of bitcoin in the exchange. Make careful to securely send the cryptocurrency you have traded back to your wallet. You want to make sure that your cryptocurrency coins are safe even if the exchange is hacked, which is why you should do this. At one time, the biggest bitcoin exchange, Mt.Gox, was hacked and declared bankruptcy. Therefore, holding your money on the exchange itself does not provide a long-term assurance of safety.

Pay great attention and only utilize the public key stored in your wallet when moving bitcoin from the exchange to the wallet (and vice versa). Never divulge or distribute your private key in front of others. even if the exchange specifically requests it.

Advice and Techniques

Tip #1: Before you start investing, choose the precise amount you want to put in. Make sure that this sum, if you're a newbie, does not exceed 5 to 10% of your whole financial resources. Your sole investment should be your surplus cash. And be ready to lose this first sum, since your initial objectives will be to test the market and try out various tactics. Additionally, if you're a beginning cryptocurrency trader, it's recommended to start with bitcoin and ethereum. Once you understand how everything works, you may contribute larger sums and try different cryptocurrencies or initial coin offerings (ICOs; we'll discuss this in a moment). However, you must constantly be aware of the hazards involved and ready for the worst case scenario.

The second piece of advice is to thoroughly research cryptocurrencies before investing. You should now have a rudimentary understanding of the cryptocurrency environment after reading this book. To understand what and where you're investing your money better, you may want to go further into the technology. Read the most recent articles, book reviews, design papers, etc. If you're a programmer, you may read the open-sourced code, which is available for public viewing. I created a different book called Bitcoin: The Digital Gold that I'd suggest to anybody interested in purchasing or investing in bitcoin if you're not a coder and want to get additional perspective. It provides in-depth explanations while taking a closer, more concentrated look at the Bitcoin network.

Third advice: Remain patient. Never purchase or sell on the basis of hype. People often succumb to the FOMO (Fear of Missing Out) phenomena when markets see significant fluctuations. At this point, you start hastily selling as the value decreases and purchasing wildly as the value increases. Despite the usual maxim of "buy low, sell high," it is always wise to use good judgment and to be on the lookout for hype rather than buying into it. The most common reason why individuals lose money while trading online is undoubtedly impatience. A man I know purchased 10 bitcoins in 2015 for around $231 and then sold them for $455. He was thrilled with the $2240 profit he had achieved. However, according to yesterday's pricing, he would have gained $32,000 if he had stayed with the bitcoins and refrained from going for the fast profit.

Fourth advice: Don't blow all of your money. Despite being so straightforward, novice traders and investors often fail at this. They generate a rapid profit and then treat themselves by buying expensive goods. That strategy when it comes to long-term wealth creation is essentially incorrect. Your profits must be set aside so that you may either utilize them as cash for your next transaction or spend them in improving your abilities and expertise.

Let's now examine some of the methods you might use to truly benefit from cryptocurrency trading or investment.

Initial Coin Offerings (ICOs)

Divide your money into 10 equal portions and put each one into 10 separate initial coin offerings. Similar to crowdsourcing, an ICO (Initial Coin Offering) allows you to participate in a firm by buying bitcoin. Contrary to real crowdsourcing, the investors' first priority is to get their money back rather than necessarily making a donation to the firm. The firm will utilize this investment as working money to complete its project(s), and if it succeeds, the cryptocurrency's value will increase significantly. The Ethereum project, which received funds originally for $0.4 per ether and is now valued at $203 with a market worth of over $19 billion, is an example of a successful ICO. Therefore, the chance of at least one of your 10 ICO investments paying off is rather high. According to bitcoin specialists, the win percentage is often about 20%. Accordingly, 2 of your 10 ICO purchases have a strong possibility of returning 10X or more. Even if you already have some bitcoins, you may use them to invest in other cryptocurrencies that have a good chance of success (during ICOs).

Second plan of attack: disruptive cryptocurrency

After you get through the learning curve of cryptocurrency investment, you'll start to focus on long-term gains. Researching and identifying the coins that are fundamentally disruptive can help you boost your chances of earning them. For instance, Bitcoin was the first digital money of its sort to provide a true decentralized currency. Similar to how smart contracts on Ethereum are upending the legal sector of business. You will ultimately be able to identify such "disruptive cryptocurrencies" if you read the white papers and do thorough study, and there is where you will have a better chance of generating long-term gains.

Third-best tactic: Buy while prices are low.

In essence, "shorting" is betting against the market. When done correctly, of course, it's not as hazardous or rebellious as it may seem. Historically, traders have made money by buying cheap and selling high. When purchasing comes first, sales follow. What if you could purchase later and sell first? Shorting operates in this manner. In essence, you borrow bitcoin or an alternative currency at first and then sell it when the price is reasonably high. After then, you monitor the market to see when the value declines. When it does, you immediately purchase back the bitcoin you sold, making a profit. The program you use automatically pays back the sum you borrowed to first sell the coins. Compared to shorting common equities on a stock market, shorting cryptocurrency carries far lower risk. Use CoinCap to see how the value of cryptocurrencies changes in real time. Remember that shorting does not perform well with long-term growths but does with short-term drops.

Is everything simply a giant bubble?

When they see how the market values are soaring or plummeting, many individuals ask this question. One of the most often used counterarguments in this context is "Well, if it's decentralized, who's gonna back it up?" The system is unsupported by any authority. Therefore, it is easy to fall into the trap of believing that cryptocurrencies are just treading water and have no firm foundation upon which to build. But nothing could be farther from the truth than this. The large user base and general acceptance of, let's say, Bitcoin, are what give it its worth. It seems sense that this is what gives something worth. public approval. not the support of a single government. The same response applies whether you look at a commodity like an Apple iPhone and ask, "Why is it worth what it's worth?" Unlike fiat currencies, which are backed by the government, iPhones are not. They are just items that a business sells that, through time and for a variety of reasons, people have learned to value highly. Therefore, cryptocurrencies gain value in the same manner that an iPhone does. public approval. They are worth more the more the people utilize them. And in terms of dependability, I believe Bitcoin's over $52 billion market valuation at the moment speaks for itself.

At this time, it is all but inevitable that over the next five years, the total market value of cryptocurrencies will hit $1 trillion. Right now, our total stands at around $111 billion. The development of cryptocurrencies and blockchain technology is inevitable given the amount of advancement being made in this industry, even in the event of a brief value decline or bubble burst. Prepare yourself for what is to come by doing so. Having said that, you will sail more easily if you adhere to some of the common sense advice presented in this chapter, diversify your money, and apply common sense.

The workings of cryptocurrencies

Transactions in a common currency, such as the British Pound or the U.S. Dollar, are carried out either by the exchange of cash or through electronic transfers. Large institutions that we trust to protect our money and maintain the integrity of our transactions are in charge of these electronic transfers.

In order to build a cryptocurrency, we must first assume control over the management of transaction records from banks. Making a ledger of everyone's payments to everyone other is the first stage. This ledger will record everyone's payments to one another and keep track of who owes whom money.

The next stage is to stop cheating by include transactions that more than one person may disagree with. Having both parties to the transaction sign off on the payment is one simple solution to that issue. Using public/private key encryption, each party may append their "digital signature" to the transaction to ensure that it is valid.

A digital signature is what? A digital signature is intended to be the equivalent of a handwritten signature on paper in the digital world. In keeping with the analogy of the handwritten signature, we want digital signatures to have two characteristics. To begin with, only you are able to create your signature, but anybody who sees it may confirm that it is legitimate. Second, we want the signature to be connected to a specific document so that it cannot be exploited to represent your agreement with or support for another paper. This last characteristic ensures that someone cannot take your handwritten signature, cut it off one document, and glue it to the bottom of another. Additionally, it is important to note that a digital signature has a foundational scheme. The following three algorithms make up a digital signature scheme:

Ethereum

This distributed computing environment will increase strangers' confidence in one another. With Ethereum, you may transact with almost anybody since all the terms and conditions are laid out in a "smart contract" that is digitally recorded on the blockchain network. The Eretheum Virtual computer [EVM], a virtual computer that checks and validates all contracts using the cryptocurrency "Ether," is provided by this smart contract feature. It is possible to employ the integrated "smart contract" more than once for various transactions. No surprise Bitcoin is the only cryptocurrency ahead of it in terms of market value as of 2017. "Ethereum: The Complete Guide To Understanding Ethereum" is available at: for a detailed look at Ethereum.

Ripple

It is also known as the Ripple Transaction Protocol (RTXP), and as might be anticipated, it is based on

Ripples (XRP), a decentralized, open-source internet protocol. All transactions, including exchanges, payments, and withdrawals, are facilitated via the Ripple protocol using an established procedure. Due to the fact that it delivers both domestically and globally quick, cost-effective payments, it is simple to comprehend and apply. It debuted in 2013.

Litecoin

The genesis of this virtual money, introduced in 2011, is very similar to that of Bitcoin. Some claim that the bitcoin served as inspiration for its inception. The transfer policy was also developed using an open source protocol. The MIT (X11) software license was used to distribute this peer-to-peer cryptocurrency.

Formerly known as Darkcoin, Dash

As indicated by its official name, Darkcoin, this digital money was introduced by Evan Duffield in 2014 and is a more covert variation of bitcoin. Because it offers additional enhanced secrecy, business interactions are practically impossible to track. The secrecy and quickness of this cryptocurrency were two of its main selling points at debut. Since then, it has exceeded expectations since "dash" has a large and loyal fan following. No one has questioned its appropriateness either.

Peercoin

Two software engineers, Scott Nadal and Sunny King, developed this unique digital money in 2012. Its combination of "proof-of-work" and "proof-of-stake" is its most distinctive characteristic. Its previous name was PPcoin. The "proof-of-work" hashing method that was first utilized to mine this currency eventually become more challenging. Users were compensated for this by receiving coins that used the "proof-of-stake" mechanism. This modified coin's benefit is that it uses less energy to create blocks, or to put it another way, to complete a transaction.

Dogecoin

This digital money, which was introduced in 2013, employs script technology as its proof-of-work mechanism. Despite significant adjustments, the structure was built on the same system that was used to create Bitcoin. This digital currency may be produced indefinitely and is best used for carrying out smaller transactions since it deals with individual coins that have lower values. There is a block time of around 60 seconds.

Primecoin

This digital money was created by software engineer Sunny King in the summer of 2013. Its proof-of-work technology, which is completely different from the Bitcoin foundation, was based on prime numbers. It aims to identify distinctive long chains of prime numbers, making mining easier and enhancing network security.

Chinacoin

You probably believe that it was produced in China or that China is the name of the developer. No. It didn't originate in China. It utilizes the same conceptual foundation as Litecoin. It makes use of the password-based script key derivation mechanism. It is created in blocks of 60 seconds, 88 coins each. Amazing!

Ven
In order to lessen the danger of inflation, this digital money was introduced in 2007. A selection of currencies, commodities, and carbon characteristics are used to calculate its worth on the financial market.

The top 10 cryptocurrencies on the market today are reviewed above, demonstrating that Bitcoin is not the only cryptocurrency. In reality, there are alternatives to the well-known Bitcoin, like Auroracoin, Mastercoin, Freicoin, Quark, Sexcoin, Namecoin, etc. There are several further varieties of digital currencies available. There are around 20 different forms of digital currencies, according to CoinMarketCap.com, a website that often reports the market capitalization of cryptocurrencies.
Improvements and Restrictions

Many people point to one limitation of this new innovation—that cryptocurrencies can only be accessed and used online—while others point to the fact that more than 40% of the world's population is unaware that digital currencies even exist as the reason why it lags behind paper money a little. However, they aren't actually major problems. Keep in mind the adage, "No Pain, No Gain"! They are only defenses rather than obstacles. Let's quickly discuss the benefits of cryptocurrencies before discussing the problems that are preventing their development.

Benefits of Cryptocurrencies

Payment Independence
With digital currencies, it is possible to send and receive money at any time from anywhere in the globe. You won't have to worry about arranging around bank holidays, crossing international borders, or any other issues that one may anticipate will arise while transferring money. With

cryptocurrencies, you are in control of your money and no third party or network central authority is required for the transaction to be completed.

Security and Control

By giving users control over their transactions, users contribute to the network's safety in the bitcoin market. Merchants are not allowed to tack on hidden fees to anything. Before imposing any fees, they must consult the customer. Without a person's personal information being connected to the transactions, payments in crypto currency may be made and completed. Cryptocurrency offers protection against identity theft and the wider issue of double spending since personal information is concealed from inquisitive eyes. To protect your money, digital currencies may be backed up and encrypted.

Immediate Closing

Real estate transactions sometimes include several third parties (lawyers, notaries), delays, and fee payments. In many aspects, the

Bitcoin/cryptocurrency blockchain is similar to a "large property rights database," according to Gallippi. For a fraction of the cost and time needed to conduct typical asset transfers, bitcoin contracts may be structured and enforced to remove or add third party approvals, reference outside facts, or be fulfilled at a future date or time.

Fraud

Because they are digital, cryptocurrencies cannot be forged or unilaterally reversed by the sender, unlike credit card charge-backs.

Transparency of Information

All completed transactions are visible to everyone using the block chain, but personal information is concealed. Your personal information is unrelated to your public address, which is what is accessible. In the blockchain of a cryptocurrency, transactions may be verified at any moment by anybody. A cryptocurrency protocol is impervious to manipulation by any individual, group, or authority. This is because digital currencies are safe in terms of cryptography. There are around 2.2 billion people without access to conventional exchange systems who have access to the Internet or mobile phones today. These people are ready to enter the cryptocurrency business. One in three Kenyans already have a bitcoin wallet, according to a recent announcement from Kenya's M-PESA system, a mobile phone-based money transfer and microfinance program.

Very Cheap Fees

Currently, costs associated with digital currency payments are either nonexistent or very little. Users may add fees to transactions in order to speed up the processing of such transactions. The faster the charge is processed, the better priority it receives throughout the network. By turning cryptocurrencies into fiat money, digital currency exchanges assist merchants in processing transactions. Generally speaking, these options have cheaper costs than PayPal and credit cards. Since the network pays the miners, cryptocurrency exchanges often don't charge transaction fees. Despite the fact that there is no transaction cost for cryptocurrencies, many anticipate that the majority of consumers will utilize a third-party service like Coinbase to create and manage their own coin wallets. These businesses provide the internet exchange mechanism for digital money, much as Paypal does for users of cash or credit cards, and as such, they are probably going to charge fees. It's noteworthy that Paypal does not receive or transmit cryptocurrency cash.

Less dangers for merchants
Merchants are shielded from any damages that may result from fraud since bitcoin transactions are safe, cannot be undone, and don't contain personal information.
With digital money, retailers may do business in areas with high crime and fraud rates. This is due to the public ledger, also known as the blockchain, which makes it incredibly difficult to

scam or defraud anybody dealing in digital currency.

Seeming Limitations or Restrictions

Cryptocurrencies have completely revolutionized the world, as seen by their exponential rise and the polarization that they have attained. According to a recent study, you would today be $10.4 million wealthier if you had known about bitcoins seven years ago and its future potential.

There are a lot of difficulties with cryptocurrencies that you should be aware of, despite their enormous potential and influence in the contemporary financial world. Let's take a quick look at these difficulties.

Absence of Knowledge & Understanding

In actuality, a lot of individuals are still ignorant about digital currencies. To be able to use cryptocurrencies in their daily lives, people must be taught about them. To spread the word about digital currencies, networking is essential. Because of its benefits, businesses now accept digital money, however the list is still rather short when compared to conventional money.

It's excellent that businesses like TigerDirect and Overstock accept digital money as payment. But how can businesses assist clients in comprehending and using digital currency for transactions if they lack qualified staff?

In order for the staff to assist the clients, they must get training on how digital currencies operate. There will undoubtedly be a time and effort commitment. If the personnel of such big businesses doesn't even understand what digital currencies are, what advantage does it serve to accept them?

Volatility and Risk

The fundamental cause of the volatility of digital currencies is that there are only a finite number of coins, and the demand for them rises daily. Though it is anticipated that the volatility would lessen with time. The price of the digital currency will ultimately stabilize as more companies, media outlets, and trade hubs start to accept it. Looking at the market right now reveals that daily price fluctuations in cryptocurrencies are mostly caused by news stories about virtual currencies.

Yet to Develop

With unfinished features still under development, digital currencies are still in their infancy. New functions, resources, and services are now being created to increase the digital currency's accessibility and security. Before reaching their ultimate and complete potential, cryptocurrencies still need to evolve. This is due to the fact that they are just getting started and must solve its challenges, just as any new currency would have to.

Nations, particularly the industrialized ones, are at war with one another right now about who gets to participate in their financial system. Numerous court lawsuits have been brought to address these issues since many countries are still not ready to verify cryptocurrencies at the state level.

Technically Difficult Aspect

Analysts and bitcoin industry experts are both worried about the Blockchain's high level of intricacy and scalability. Due to multiple scalability problems, including bandwidth TPS (transactions per second), DDoS assaults, and Blockchain size, if these digital currencies continue to gain popularity, there is a chance that the whole system may crash. To ensure the success and long-term viability of cryptocurrencies, a strong infrastructure must be put in place to guard against such occurrences.

Building Blocks of Consensus

Proof-of-work (PoW) often causes a concentration of mining and technology. Additionally, attackers have a fantastic chance to keep up parallel block chains without having to pay a lot of money thanks to Proof-of-stake (PoS).

The fact that some individuals worry that their security is in jeopardy since the network makes all transactions public must also be mentioned. Some people wonder whether their keys' security, particularly their private keys, will ever be compromised. Do you also have it on your mind? This topic will be covered in greater detail under the heading "Wallets." There is really nothing to be concerned about as long as you have a reliable method of remembering or recovering your passwords and safeguarding your machine from viruses.

The global viability of cryptocurrencies is seriously threatened by these issues. As we continue to invest in different cryptocurrencies, there are more difficulties that we need to be aware of, like the hypervolatility and unanticipated growth in digital currency costs.

High rates are the outcome of a limited supply, and value is inversely proportional to market demand. It is also crucial to remember that, particularly when evaluating digital currency, it is impossible to implement any kind of quantitative easing since the coins are only made accessible at the speed at which the processing networks involved can resolve blocks. Despite these difficulties, the value of different cryptocurrencies has increased significantly, mainly to improvements made to the systems that are used to keep track of them.

Success may be far off without certain sacrifices, as we already noted. All of today's well-known figures had humble beginnings, and what they fail to mention is how many times they fell and got back up. You don't have to worry about "falling down" with cryptocurrency. The sky is not just the limit but also your starting point if you have all the information and are aware of what to anticipate.

Uses for cryptocurrencies

facilitating access to necessities Lack of money in developing nations results in a lack of access to necessities like insurance and health care. More money is needed than they earn in order to access these services. Additionally, insurers often take advantage of these low-wage workers by diverting their funds and raising the premiums unduly. By limiting these activities to an online setting, cryptocurrency will lessen the effects of the dishonest insurer. Additionally, it will allow clients to make lesser payments.

affordable money transfers The fact that cryptocurrency has a very cheap transaction cost when compared to other electronic payment systems is one of its main advantages. Compared to the costs on money transfers facilitated by banks, credit cards, and commercial technologies like PayPal, the minimal transaction charge is very cheap. The reduced prices of digital currency transactions are particularly helpful for immigrants who transfer money back to their family back home. Simply because the remittance transfer market is extremely vast (remittance flows were $542 billion worldwide in 2013), this is a major potential market for cryptocurrencies. International transfers may be quite costly; in fact, the average price for such payments globally during the first quarter of 2015 was 7.72%, according to the World Bank's report on Remission Prices. An estimated $442 billion was transferred to families in less developed nations by those living in rich nations last year. They want to improve their lives, therefore we can't criticize this. Without a question, we all wish to support our struggling family. However, can you attempt to calculate how much cash is required to send such a huge sum of money? We are all aware that companies like MoneyGram, Western Union money transfer, and others in this category charge for their services when sending money. However, by employing digitalized digital currencies for such payments, you may avoid paying bank fees and following standard remittance processes. More money will be sent home and saved. Additionally, it may take a long time for the brokering banking institutions to verify such payments. With the help of cryptocurrencies like Bitcoin, immigrants may transmit payments cheaply and almost immediately. The average transaction fee was 0.000155 BTC as of April 2015 (about $0.04 per transaction at the time). The interval between transaction blocks was 9.11 minutes on average.

Managing private expenses: One of the main benefits of cryptocurrencies is their pseudonymous nature, which allows for member identification through their public keys rather than their "real world" identities. This provides a degree of anonymity that many individuals seek that typical digital payment methods do not. People who are escaping violent spouses, wanting debatable medical treatments, or acting independently of authoritarian regimes are a few instances of scenarios in which this attribute truly comes into play. Unfortunately, there is a downside to this secrecy, which is that cryptocurrencies may be utilized for immoral and illegal activities. The notorious "Deep Web" bazaar Silk Road is the most known illustration of this. Users may purchase and trade illegal goods on Silk Road because to the secrecy offered by cryptocurrencies and an anonymous program called TOR. Users may still buy unlawfully produced products including illegal narcotics and fraudulent identification cards even if Silk Road's moderators forbade the selling of commodities that were produced or intended to cause the damage or exploitation of other people. The greater anonymity of digital currency may also provide criminals a way to launder money or support terrorist groups.

Day-to-day purchases – While the aforementioned applications are niche ones, the typical cryptocurrency user will only use it to make regular purchases from online (or even offline) merchants. This will happen more often as the cryptocurrency market expands; customers will want to spend their virtual money, businesses will gain from accepting it, and the value of cryptocurrencies will (theoretically) stabilize. There are a few reasons why this is a good development. First off, the previously stated low transaction costs are a fantastic incentive for companies to take digital currency as payment; by lowering the fees associated with credit card transactions, authorizations, statements, interchanges, and customer service fees, retailers can dramatically minimize their expenses. Second, the use of digital currency makes the new payment system a catalyst for financial innovation. Elements like micropayments, which are typically not supported by other financial systems, open up new financial opportunities and encourage the development of new online business models and marketing techniques.

Application in Banking: A large number of major banks are testing the use of digital currencies to streamline and modernize banking procedures while reducing expenses. The potential to develop novel business models and the probability of competing with fintechs are two additional motivations for trying it out. They are also investigating how digital currencies may assist in resolving various issues that their firms deal with on a daily basis. The framework's usage by banking regulatory bodies is another effort to create more effective rules. In reality, it will help transactions move more quickly and protect them.

Major financial industries began to consider blockchain technology, the engine behind all cryptocurrencies, in 2015. It was also emphasized that collaboration and partnerships throughout the sector are essential if financial institutions like the Banks are to successfully use this technology. The fact that the crypto-cash technology will aid in resolving several significant issues with the banking system was also underlined. problems such as:
avoiding tampering with an established sequence of transactions.
The problem of double dipping
issues involving trust
agreement on the history of transactions
Another aspect of this technology that will help both clients and the financial system is transparency. No record will be able to be changed by anybody. In fact, by 2022, it may have saved the

infrastructure of banks $20 billion annually.

Today, centralized systems that maintain their own central ledgers are often used to verify transactions. The days it may take to conclude an agreement might slow down transactions. Additionally, it may take days for two or more institutions to compare and concur on the data of a certain consumer. However, the digital currency proposal will do away with that waiting time as each bank would get a copy of the ledger as soon as the transactions are submitted. Participants will be able to communicate easily as a result. Transactions will be verified instantly, resulting in considerable cost savings.

The marketing industry will change as well. Today, many marketing processes could include the use of middlemen, several handoffs, drawn-out processes, and the like. But the use of cryptocurrencies will solve all of these issues. The usage of "smart contracts" is another feature of digital currency that is worth mentioning. As long as certain requirements are satisfied, this will generate a transaction path where certain activities will be authorized automatically. Remittances will be accepted, for instance, provided that certain codes are full.

Digital Identity Security Any area of human effort, including employment, business, pleasure, politics, and healthcare, is closely related to permission of identities. However, there are issues with the idea of identity authorisation, maybe due to poor common grasp and the mostly unregulated internet of personal data. Recent technological advancements, such as the rise in instances of breached accounts and database hacks, represent a danger to digital identities. Cryptocurrency uses biometrics to address these challenges with digital identification, allowing for the unique authorization of identities in a way that is unchangeable, indisputable, and secure.

So how precisely can digital currencies contribute to the safety of digital identity? We must first think about how digital identities are represented in the blockchain network (already discussed) in order to comprehend that. The blockchain network interprets a user's identification as a self-asserted block containing the user's identity characteristic. The user's private and public keys are also included in the block. In addition, banks or power suppliers' public keys or pins for validation are included in the user's block of data.

By logging in with the public keys, the user's connection to the electrical service provider is created. As more of these connections are made inside the blockchain network, the trust in the veracity of the user's identity rises naturally. Gradually, further connections are made between the user and the connected suppliers. The'reputation capital' of the user's identity also increases steadily as more transactions are carried out in their name.

The blockchain records any changes to one or more of the relationships between the user and the entities as a separate block with a distinctive cryptographically signed timestamp. By doing so, a cryptographically protected sequence is produced that the new verifier may use to match up connections between the past and present.

Real estate application Individuals or businesses will be able to transfer information, money, or other types of assets rapidly and without the need for middlemen thanks to the blockchain technology that underpins all cryptocurrencies. They may also be used to easily transfer assets in real estate. We'll now look at three potential ways that using cryptocurrencies can either make real estate better or completely alter it.

A smart contract.

Disintermediation

Defending against fraud

Let's talk about each one in turn now.

Intelligent Contracts The smart contract seems to be one of the better aspects of digital money since it has been shown to be helpful in many different contexts. With it, there won't be any more instances when one side complies with their commitments while the other one does not. It is automatic because the agreement will remain in effect as long as specific requirements are satisfied by both parties. As an example, imagine being paid as soon as you hit a particular percentage of the customer base. As scams become extinct due to transparency, there would be fewer court proceedings.

Disintermediation: When third parties or intermediaries are involved or necessary to make the negotiations fall through, real estate transactions may get problematic. These third parties might be escrow firms, stock brokers, inspectors, appraisers, or in certain situations even governmental organizations. These transactions will be delayed for a number of days while the middlemen finish out their work, which may be expensive and wasteful of precious time. It seems as if we rely on them to make the transactions happen. Why are intermediaries required in real estate transactions? Why is it necessary for them to certify our title deeds and other paperwork? It is because they possess knowledge, credentials, and access to certain information that we lack. These credentials and information are necessary for these transactions to fail. As is well known, blockchain technology is a public digital record that allows simultaneous access to everyone connected without the requirement for any kind of authorization or information withholding. It implies that every property will be capable of managing transactions on their own whenever necessary without the help of a third party.

Let's use TITLE as an example; at the moment, a property's title is nothing more than a piece of paper. The document must be carefully completed, signed with a pen if necessary, and then the middleman, a notary, almost certainly rubber stamps it. The county recorder then manually enters it into their database. When you consider the whole procedure, you'll see how much time and money will be lost trying to enter it into the database. But here is where using digital money may be beneficial and greatly simplify the procedures. It will take the role of a paper title, and a digital title will be produced using a cryptocurrency like Bitcoin. Then, it may be quickly sent online to the required authorities, eliminating the requirement for a third party and thus saving a lot of time.

Defending against fraud The issue of fraud is a big one in the world of commerce. Everyone wants to get fast money, therefore they use all kinds of methods to do it, including falsifying documents and data, misrepresenting bank receipts and statements, deeds, and driver's licenses, all in an effort to increase their income. Another widespread crime is real estate fraud, which is alarmingly on the rise in recent years. Even the biggest and safest banks in the world sometimes become victims of such illicit activity. But how can blockchain technology stop these nefarious real estate activities? The chief executive officer of a London-based IT company, Don Oparah, has the following to say on how blockchain can enhance real estate transactions: "By providing a resource that is completely impervious to corruption, allowing senders and recipients of payments to be tracked, and storing digital ownership certificates for properties, the blockchain might easily put an end to falsified ownership of papers and misleading listings. A property in the system would be immediately connected to each individual digital ownership of a certificate, making it impossible to sell or advertise properties you do not really possess. It follows that blockchain technology will significantly minimize fraud in real estate transactions.

Assistance to Small Businesses: Some firms may find it very difficult to qualify for and get authorized for a loan in these developing countries. This is due to the fact that intermediaries play a significant role in these nations' credit availability. In addition to that, these loans have very high interest rates even though they are difficult to get. Additionally, banks reject requests for loans in regions with a history of fraud and corruption. However, the invention of digital currencies will assist in eliminating the function of these intermediaries; it will encourage openness, which will lessen fraudulent actions. Small enterprises will be able to expand their markets and get financing in this manner.

Offering Relief Non-governmental groups and foreign businesses in wealthier nations sometimes donate money, clothing, and other supplies to these developing nations, particularly when a tragedy hits. Due to fraud and poor administration, it often transpires that humanitarian aid is not used for its intended goals. The expense of shipping these aid supplies to these target nations is another obstacle. The usage of cryptocurrencies for this kind of charitable contributions may be very beneficial in two ways: it will save the cost of shipping them and will maintain track of how these humanitarian goods are utilised. Donors may truly trust that their wishes for the use of their funds will be honored and followed.

Cryptocurrency storage: digital wallets
I'll say congrats if you're considering investing in the cryptocurrency industry. The location of all those glittering electronic currencies is the next thing you should think about. You may store and manage your bitcoin accounts in a number of ways; logically, the tools created to do so are referred to as wallets. In actuality, it's really hard to have a cryptocurrency account without a wallet connected to it.

Your standard wallet serves as a storage space for your financial instruments in addition to serving as a location to hold family photos, ticket stubs, and anything else may accumulate inside. Most individuals store their ordinary bill and coin money, credit cards, and bank cards in their wallets. A bitcoin wallet isn't that much different, however. They exist in four distinct varieties and are designed to hold all the data relevant to your digital currency account.

Program Wallets. These are software that are installed on a desktop or laptop computer for account access and maintenance, ranging from very basic simplicity to extremely vast and complicated applications. Software wallets sometimes include extra features like market graphs and mining software as space is less of a concern than it is with mobile wallets (please see below). Now let's look at several software wallets that are suggested for ease of usage.

Bitcoin-Qt: It is possible to store solely Bitcoin (a kind of digital cash) with this initial Bitcoin client. Of all software wallets, it boasts the best levels of security, privacy, and stability. The fact that it has fewer features and takes up so much space on your computer is the sole drawback.

Armory: Armory is a cutting-edge Bitcoin client that, as its name implies, is security software. For power users, it includes more functions. It provides encryption methods, cold storage on offline machines, and backup functions.

Multibit: It is lighter than bitcoin-Qt and is similar to it. Its primary goals are speed and usability. It synchronizes with the Bitcoin network, and after a short period of time, it is operational. It is the ideal option for those who have no interest in technology since it supports a wide range of languages.

Electrum is a unique software wallet that emphasizes efficiency and ease of use. Many people prefer it since it doesn't take up a lot of space or resources on your computer. The majority of the challenging components of any cryptocurrency system are handled by distant servers.

The following 2 security precautions in respect to software wallets may assist you in safeguarding your funds.

Encrypting your wallet will protect it from viruses and hackers. Any time this wallet has to be accessed, a password must be supplied in order to decrypt it and allow for transaction processing. This will also safeguard the "wallet.dat" file, which has your private key. Although it is still not completely secure since certain powerful tools, such as keylogs, may be used to decipher your passwords. Because of this, experts advise that you have a variety of Bitcoin wallets. Additionally, they advise against keeping a lot of bitcoins in a single wallet. You may store some money in your software wallet and put a lot of money in your paper wallet.

Backing up your wallet is a wise precaution to take in case your computer fails. We all appreciate making backups of our data since we never know when our computer may act up. How much more our Bitcoin wallet, which houses our money, if we can do that with files. We may secure our wallet in a variety of methods. While some people have chosen to utilize online cloud backups, we may use external hard drives. Just keep in mind that there is a possibility of Mobile Wallet hacking with any online backup. You may use these portable applications on your smartphone or tablet anywhere. For investors who like making purchases on the fly, they are perfect. These are often smaller and easier to use apps than software wallets because of the space restrictions that come with mobile devices.

Online wallets. This kind of wallet, which utilizes cloud computing and can be accessed from any computer device, is provided by currency exchangers. A trade-off with web wallets is that although they are easier to use, the internet accessibility of digital currency information might result in hacking and theft.

Either cold storage or paper wallets. You may print out the codes for your money, which can then be kept in a conventional wallet alongside traditional bills and coins. These are perfect for traders who want to spend the majority of their cryptocurrencies for investments rather than purchases. In compared to their digital relatives, paper wallets provide investors a very high degree of security—provided they are securely secured under lock and key.

Additionally, there are "hybrid" wallets, which combine the global accessibility of online wallets with the local storage capacities of software wallets. Since they need the installation of a program on a computer device, the majority of experts in the area of digital currencies classify hybrid wallets as improved software wallets.

After looking more closely at the different kinds of wallets available to investors as well as some suggestions for consideration when looking around for a wallet, it is crucial to remember that you can transfer your cryptocurrency funds without any hassle from one wallet to another. For instance, several currencies—and exchanges as well—offer their recommended wallets upon registration or first deposit. Most of the time, you are free to browse around elsewhere to locate a wallet that more closely meets your personal requirements; only in exceptional circumstances are you compelled to choose the wallet given in these situations.

In light of this, there is a wallet out there that is perfect for you, whether you only need space for your account or one with all the bells and whistles. We'll also provide some advice to bear in mind when it comes to protecting your bitcoin investment as many wallet features deal with security. You probably already know that wallet hacks may result in a complete loss, thus security is essential for your investment.

Investors have a wide selection of options for storing and maintaining their digital currency accounts. This section has served as a resource to help you comprehend the idea of a cryptocurrency wallet as well as what buyers should look for in order to discover one that works with their buying and investment goals. Your wallet effectively serves as your alternative currency account, and the latter relies on the former in order to operate. Therefore, you don't have to be concerned about losing money while you keep your bitcoin for usage in the future. There are currently few online wallets that provide sufficient protection to be used to hold assets similarly to a bank. The ability to utilize cryptocurrencies anywhere with less effort to secure your wallets is one benefit of the online wallet. However, online wallets have a strong future since they are likely to become more secure over time.

It actually depends on how you want to use your digital money as to how you chose to keep it. It will be preferable to retain the majority of your digital currency in cold storage or a paper wallet if you want to make long-term investments. The software wallet is your best choice if you want to make a quick and easy investment. The online wallet and mobile wallet are what you need if you want to swap digital currencies quickly.

Summary

If someone wants to persuade me to try a new food, they should describe what I will like about it in order to pique my interest. This chapter has made an effort to do that. Discussing the many forms of cryptocurrencies that are now causing a stir in the market, as well as what makes them unique and how they function (Mechanics). Additionally, we have seen the different ways that using digital currency might benefit people in general, both now and in the future. It has also been beneficial to examine the obstacles preventing its expansion and contrast its benefits. Finally, the idea of digital wallets and advice for keeping virtual currency were discussed. We'll examine the process of developing new cryptocurrencies and how this project will alter the nature of the global economy in the next chapter.

Cryptocurrency Trading and Investment

You must first understand how to store and purchase cryptocurrencies before you can invest in or trade them. We will use the example of Bitcoin to clarify the procedure as almost all cryptocurrencies are stored, acquired, and sold in the same way.

Step 1: Purchasing

Bitcoins are most often acquired via computer mining. Even while it's not the simplest or cheapest method, it does enable you to profit from your mining activities by receiving free Bitcoin. It is a set of challenging mathematical problems that computers solve. This is how the first Bitcoins were produced, and this is also how new ones are continuously produced. Using these sophisticated computers and their mathematical algorithms, around 25 Bitcoins are mined every 10 minutes as of the time of this publishing.

Finding a Bitcoin exchange and buying Bitcoins there is another far simpler approach to get your hands on them. Due to the prevalence of these exchanges and the peculiarities of the currency, it is crucial that you take your time and choose a trustworthy exchange. Avoid any business or person that offers to assist you in mining bitcoin, anything that appears too good to be true, and anything that just seems off. Ideally, you should be able to look up the specific Bitcoin exchange and quickly find out a lot of information about it. Always do your homework before making an exchange to be sure you are not being taken advantage of. Because Bitcoin is so valuable right now, many people are taking advantage of it to defraud others of their money, and you do not want to fall for this. Pyramid schemes using Bitcoin are a further point worth mentioning. Despite the fact that they may seem beneficial or like they will help you with your investments, they won't allow you to save money, and it's probable that you won't end up with any Bitcoin.

Despite the fact that there are several Bitcoin scams out there, it's crucial to realize that this is not a reason to fully give up on the cryptocurrency. Remember that although being very valued and even necessary to daily living in our culture, conventional currencies may nonetheless lead to frauds. Bitcoins are still quite valuable and may provide significant returns and riches to people who buy or invest in them, even if they are not as essential to our everyday lives as other commodities.

The best course of action is to make sure that the sites you use to get your Bitcoin are reliable and legal. You may easily start investing in as much Bitcoin as you like after you've found a reliable exchange to do it on. This is the simplest and safest method to invest in Bitcoin ownership and trading without having to worry about being duped or otherwise taken advantage of in the cryptocurrency world.

Exchanging cryptocurrencies

An online platform known as a cryptocurrency exchange allows users to purchase, trade, and swap one cryptocurrency for another or for traditional fiat money like dollars and pounds. various cryptocurrency exchanges cater to various types of customers depending on their individual demands.

There are sophisticated exchanges that enable you to trade professionally and have access to sophisticated trading tools. Before you can create a trading account on the majority of them, you will often need to authenticate your identification. There are straightforward exchanges that enable you to trade without needing to set up a trading account for individuals searching for a one-time or seldom deal.

Three different categories of bitcoin exchanges exist:

• Trading platforms: These systems link traders and tack on a fee for each exchange. They serve as escrow, managing the processing of orders and transactions while keeping both cryptocurrency and fiat currency.

- Direct trading platforms: Peer-to-peer marketplaces are another name for them. Direct trading platforms, as opposed to trading platforms, let buyers and sellers conduct transactions directly. Platforms for direct trading lack a set market price. Exchange rates are set by sellers.
- Websites that function similarly to foreign currency brokers include brokers and direct commercial exchanges. They make it simple for anybody to purchase bitcoins at pre-set rates set by the exchange.

Selecting a Trade

Those who wish to start trading cryptocurrencies have access to a number of exchanges. But you shouldn't sign up for an exchange just because it was the first one you came across. Keep the following things in mind before participating in an exchange.

Reputation: The first step you should do when thinking about a certain exchange is to look through evaluations from users as well as from official industry sources. Ask any questions you may have regarding an exchange by visiting online groups and forums where cryptocurrency aficionados congregate.

Fees: Transaction, deposit, and withdrawal fees are assessed to users by cryptocurrency exchanges. This is what sustains their operations. The charge schemes vary across exchanges. The majority of popular exchanges have a volume-based pricing system that lets users who do a lot of transactions pay lesser costs. Make sure you are completely familiar with the exchange's cost structure before joining. The website of the exchange has the majority of this information readily available.

Payment options: Research the various payment options before signing up for a platform to determine whether they suit your needs. Keep in mind that using PayPal and credit cards can result in additional fees, and receiving your bitcoin via a bank transfer may need more time.

Most bitcoin exchanges in the U.S. and U.K. have verification requirements. some will demand identification confirmation prior to a person being able to deposit and withdraw money, while others provide total anonymity. Verification helps safeguard the exchange against money laundering and frauds, despite the fact that it may appear to go against the spirit of cryptocurrency.

Geographical limitations: Some exchanges could include features that are only usable from inside certain geographical areas or nations. Verify if the exchange gives complete assistance in your nation before signing up.

Exchange rates: The exchange rates for cryptocurrencies vary across exchanges. To determine which exchange gives the best price for the cryptocurrency you want to trade, compare several marketplaces.

Various Exchanges

The top five cryptocurrency exchanges are discussed here, taking into account customer feedback, security, fee structures, accessibility, and user friendliness.

Coinbase

One of the most well-known bitcoin exchanges worldwide is this one. It was founded in 2012, has a solid track record, reliable investor support, and millions of users. The Coinbase platform is incredibly easy and user-friendly, enabling users to purchase, sell, store, and spend bitcoins in a safe manner. Bitcoin, Ether, and Litecoin are supported by Coinbase. Additionally, it offers a mobile wallet that works on both iOS and Android devices. Through a mobile wallet or by trading with other users on the Global Digital Asset Exchange (GDAX), a division of Coinbase, customers may buy cryptocurrencies. The nicest things about Coinbase are its excellent security, affordable fees, and user-friendliness. The Coinbase insurance also applies to funds kept on the platform. However, Coinbase's GDAX platform is better suited to technical users, and it only supports a small number of countries and payment options.

Kraken

This 2011-founded exchange has its headquarters in San Francisco. The first bitcoin bank in the world will be created thanks to a partnership between Kraken and Fidor. It is integrated with Bloomberg terminals as well. Users have access to a broad range of international currencies, including U.S. dollars, Canadian dollars, British pounds, euros, and Japanese yen, via Kraken. Numerous other virtual currencies are also supported by Kraken, including as Bitcoin, Ethereum, Ethereum Classic, Ripple, Dogecoin, Monero, Litecoin, Stellar, Zcash, and ICONOMI. The reasons Kraken is so well-known are its sterling reputation, reasonable deposit and transaction fees, respectable exchange rates, wealth of features, global support, and excellent customer assistance. Limited payment options and a confusing user interface are some of its shortcomings, making it less than ideal for beginners.

Poloniex

Since its establishment in 2014, Poloniex has developed into one of the largest cryptocurrency exchanges in the world. It enables trades between Bitcoin and more than 100 other cryptocurrencies. Poloniex's account creation process is quick and easy. The platform has a feature-rich, intuitive user interface and provides additional analytical capabilities for individuals with greater experience. One of the most affordable bitcoin exchanges is Poloniex. With a chat interface where users may ask for assistance from other users, user support is excellent. The discussion box is kept useful by moderators who remove any offensive remarks. Additionally providing BTC financing, Poloniex also provides an open API. The lack of support for fiat currencies on Poloniex is a drawback.

Shapeshift

Shapeshift is a real-time cryptocurrency exchange that was established in 2013 that lets customers trade one cryptocurrency for another. Bitcoin and a number of other cryptocurrencies, such as Ethereum, Dash, Dogecoin, Monero, and Zcash, are supported by Shapeshift. Sadly, Shapeshift does not support bitcoin and fiat trades. Shapeshift's ability to facilitate cryptocurrency exchanges while preserving a high degree of anonymity is one of its key benefits. Users do not need to register for an account to swap bitcoins. Even its holdings on a central exchange are nonexistent. Shapeshift has a solid reputation, an easy-to-use interface, affordable fees, and it supports several cryptocurrencies.

LocalBitcoins

With support for thousands of cities worldwide, this well-known P2P marketplace links Bitcoin merchants and consumers inside the same city or geographical area. With LocalBitcoins, the parties to the transaction may agree on their preferred method of payment or even meet in person. While charging a 1% charge for each deal, the site lets sellers choose their own exchange rates. It employs a reputation rating system and keeps a public history of each user's transactions to protect the platform's security. Additionally, it offers an escrow service that retains money and only releases them after the seller confirms that the transaction is complete. On LocalBitcoins, there is no need to verify your identity before signing up. It offers a free, user-friendly solution for beginners to buy bitcoins, supports different local currencies depending on where you are, and is accessible anywhere. Its disadvantage is that it has expensive exchange rates, making it a poor choice for purchasing significant quantities of Bitcoin.

2nd step: storing

Similar to regular money, you hold Bitcoins in a digital "wallet" of sorts. When you make your first Bitcoin purchase, a wallet is automatically established and maintained for you going forward. You may add Bitcoin to your digital wallet whenever you buy it or make an investment in it. Similar to this, each time you spend money, money will be taken out of this digital wallet.

Either on your computer or in a cloud storage system is where your digital wallet may be found. This wallet functions precisely as your bank would, keeping track of each Bitcoin you add and remove. This wallet may be used to aid you in making purchases, receiving or transferring money, or even storing your Bitcoin cash.

It's crucial to realize, however, that there are certain risks associated with using your digital wallet that, should they occur, cannot be reversed. For instance, because the wallet is not covered by the FDIC's insurance, you will not be able to recover or revive your money if you have any inconsistencies or lose any of them. There are further considerations to make about the location of the wallet as well. Some businesses may have the authority to take more Bitcoin than you have authorized or to otherwise take your money from cloud-based wallets. Additionally, servers might be compromised, and the hacker could take your Bitcoin. However, if you keep your wallet on your computer, it may be hacked, get infected with viruses, or it might get erased or lost if your computer ever breaks down.

3rd step: trading

Nasdaq will start trading Bitcoin in 2018, opening a new era in the development of cryptocurrencies. Trading will be especially profitable for those who were prepared to stick with it through the volatile price fluctuations that the coins exhibit. Generally speaking, one should purchase when prices are low and sell when they are high. Due to the day-to-day volatility of the prices, traders may execute hundreds of deals in a single 24-hour period. Many people have discovered that they are generating substantial amounts of money.

You need to choose the cryptocurrencies you wish to utilize before you can begin trading. Some traders solely work with a single cryptocurrency, basing all of their transactions on the profits and losses of that currency. Others exchange cryptocurrency in order to profit from market patterns across the whole crypto-economy. Additionally, you'll need to choose a trading platform and your preferred tactics. The best method to learn the best trading strategies is to start off by working with an experienced trader until you get the feel of it.

Step 4: Earning Cash

This section will look at the many methods you may make money using cryptocurrencies. Making money with cryptocurrencies is not especially difficult.

allowing payment with cryptocurrency

You may ask for payments in cryptocurrency from others if you are in a position to accept cash from them. You may accept bitcoin payments whether you run a brick-and-mortar shop or an internet company. You may utilize applications to make them available. Because you let customers pay as they want to, you could discover that more individuals are eager to support your company. Perhaps your relatives or friends are willing to give you some money. You have the option of asking for it to be sent to you in bitcoin. All you have to do is provide them the address for your account.

Mining

The method through which new bitcoin tokens are produced is called mining. To validate the transactions in a block of transactions, a challenging mathematical challenge must be solved. These riddles are solved by miners using their computers. After then, new tokens are produced, some of which are often awarded as rewards to the miner who cracked the code.

You will need a strong computer, some specialized gear and software, as well as a cheap source of electricity, to start mining. Because mining uses a lot of energy and might rapidly lose money, you want inexpensive energy. The value of whatever advances you make won't be negated if you have a consistent supply of wind, solar, or another renewable energy source.

You must carefully choose the cryptocurrency you want to mine before you begin mining. Individuals can no longer make money mining Bitcoins since the equipment has become so costly due to technical advancements. Other cryptocurrencies, such the LSK and Dash, have distinct mining algorithms that only allow specific users to mine. The majority of Bitcoin mining is done on so-called "mining farms." You must be a respected member of the community and get nomination in order to mine LSK. The "mining elite" and more "common" miners are the two groups into which Dash has separated the mining process. This will guarantee the quick transaction times Dash guarantees.

Other cryptocurrencies like Dogecoin and Ether are simple for anybody to mine. There isn't much motivation to develop ever-more-advanced hardware since Dogecoin isn't extremely lucrative and is seen as having a more enjoyable, humorous culture. As a consequence, the only equipment needed is a computer with plenty of memory, a steady Internet connection, and a cheap energy supply. Anyone may mine ethereum. Companies are motivated to develop more potent mining gear because it has become so lucrative. As a consequence, mining Ether can become more costly over time.

Joining a mining pool is an option to mine alone with your own computer. A collection of users that pool their computing resources to solve the block hashes more quickly and increase their chances of winning rewards is known as a mining pool. The awards are then distributed among the many mining pool participants, based on the amount of power they provided.

the production of one's own cryptocurrency

Making your own cryptocurrency is another method to make money with them! On the blockchain of the website, Counterparty enables anybody to establish their own coin.

The mere act of creating a coin does not guarantee financial success. The majority of cryptocurrencies appear and go without ever appreciating in value. Remember that in order for money to have worth, people must desire it. They must think it is valuable in order for them to demand it. Long before Bitcoin's value skyrocketed in terms of money, it had worth in the form of social capital. Because they agreed with its idea, people started to want it; the increase in value followed.

Making a cryptocurrency for no other reason than for enjoyment, then waiting for it to take off, is most likely doomed to failure. Your mother and your closest friend may purchase $10 worth, which might not even be enough to pay your early costs.

Make your cryptocurrency a component of a software that users will want to use in its place. Think about creating a dapp on Lisk, Blockstack, or Ethereum. You'll need to think of a commercial concept to do this. A digital application called Augur enables users to make predictions, which improves the accuracy of future event forecasting. FirstBlood is a dapp that allows users to gamble on e-sports without the usual corruption that afflicts the sector. Alice.si keeps charities responsible by forcing them to complete certain requirements prior to receiving donations. All of these dApps fill a certain need, which encourages users to utilize them.

Advantages and Drawbacks of Investing

Advantages

The largest benefit that Bitcoin has to provide is payment independence. For consumers wishing to make purchases from an overseas merchant, the ability to conduct international transactions without interruption from the government, holidays, banks, or other disruptions is an amazing feature that dramatically speeds up performing transactions.

The freedom to select your own costs is another perk. When using your Bitcoins to complete transactions, you are free to choose to pay any amount, even zero. Your costs only have an impact on how quickly the transaction is completed.

Customers and businesses are both protected while using Bitcoin because of its anonymity. The transactions are final, so a client cannot pay for something, get it, then go back and reverse the transaction to get their money back. Believe it or not, many users of debit cards and credit cards employ this common scamming technique. Blockchain, a technology used by Bitcoin, permanently records the transaction, making it irreversible. Additionally, being anonymous implies that any sensitive data related to the transaction—including that of the customer and the merchant—is totally concealed. The blockchain permanently stores just the transaction's essential details.

Disadvantages

Despite the fact that Bitcoin is a fantastic form of money, it still has a lot of drawbacks. Their usefulness and effectiveness for individuals who choose to employ them are both slightly impacted by these drawbacks.

The degree of acceptance is the first and largest drawback. Even while the number of businesses accepting Bitcoin payments is expanding quickly, it is still not as commonly accepted as conventional money. This implies that, despite the fact that in principle everything should function flawlessly, you are unable to utilize your Bitcoin anyplace. The more this list expands, the more the network will profit from it and the more probable it is that the value of Bitcoin will continue to rise since supply and demand will inevitably rise.

The volatility of Bitcoin is another factor that makes it not always the greatest currency to invest in. It may be quite challenging to use Bitcoin since the value is still much below what it might be and is changing quickly. Based only on volatility, you can have a certain worth one day and much less the next. Utilizing them as a result might be unexpected and annoying.

Investing Advice and Techniques

There are several guidelines you should follow while investing, some more crucial than others.

The first is the longevity rule. Long-term investment gives you the ability to protect against short-term swings in very turbulent markets. You can lower risks as an investment thanks to this. Depending on the sort of investor you are, you may benefit from the cryptocurrency market's high volatility, but you might also lose a lot of money. It is strongly advised to consider the long-term potential. You must pick initiatives that have this when making a long-term investment; you must look at both the product and the people who made it. You must be aware of the investment you are making and consider if there will be a need for or use of the service in the future. Is there any rivalry that this project won't be able to easily beat? Do the creators exhibit dedication? There is a significant amount of risk involved until you know what you are really investing in.

The second guideline is to never make an investment in a company you don't fully comprehend. You will be a part of an emotional rollercoaster if you don't believe in the initiative. Prices for cryptocurrencies often fluctuate up and down. You won't worry when prices decline if you are confident in the project and know what you're investing in. In order to decide if a project is worthy of consideration or not, you need concentrate on the following three factors:

• An existing or rising demand for it — A project has to have a commercial value in order to be worthwhile. The project's demand will decide this. Even if you believe something is incredible, if no one else agrees, it has no actual worth. When initially beginning out, think about looking at cryptocurrencies in the Top 10 Market Capitalization. There are many interesting initiatives. Go to coinmarketcap.com.

• There is no significant competition Any significant competition will limit the project's potential expansion. Since several cryptocurrencies use the same concepts, the lack of innovation will cause the market to become more competitive.

Developers who are dedicated - Knowing who is in control of operations is crucial when investing in anything, whether businesses, cryptocurrencies, or stocks. The firm will advance more quickly under strong executives. Elon Musk of Tesla and SpaceX, as well as Steve Jobs of Apple, are two excellent examples. A notable example of a cryptocurrency entrepreneur is Charlie Lee of Litecoin or Vitalik Buterin, the creator of Ethereum.

Focusing on the platform rather than simply the features is the third guideline. This is crucial since many of the existing cryptocurrency initiatives are just full of features and don't provide a meaningful platform. You may wonder just what a platform is. A cryptocurrency platform is one that offers a wide range of services. In other words, it accomplishes or makes possible something other than serving as electronic money. Some cryptocurrencies are targeted for a specific market, such gambling or marijuana legalization.

Since there are now approximately 20 to 30 viable cryptocurrency ventures, the hundreds of others are not very useful as long-term investments. Platforms are cryptocurrencies with a lot of momentum and support, like Bitcoin or Ethereum.

Compare a cryptocurrency to the major cryptocurrency exchanges like Bitcoin or Ethereum while evaluating it. Do you think the project stacks up well? Does the initiative have a track record and a solid foundation? If not, it is most likely not a wise long-term investment.

The potential of the initiatives determines the long-term values of cryptocurrencies. Smaller projects thus have less potential and are less likely to increase in value over time.

How is blockchain technology being used by businesses?

Blockchain and distributed ledger technology implementation projects have grown dramatically in recent years. These technologies, which have historically been connected to cryptocurrencies and, more broadly, with the exchange of value (the Internet of Value), are now used in a variety of fields, from the financial industry to government and public sector projects. In reality, businesses and PA are beginning to grasp the advantages of these technologies and to collaborate on the creation of specific initiatives.

the uses of blockchain

There have been several books published on what can be done with blockchain, but it is difficult to get beyond the basic definition. The most immediate possibilities for the market are in financial transactions, document certification, digital identity, and cybersecurity. The real use cases are already here, such as the traceability of people and objects, intellectual property, or virtual banking.

What comes next? Any organization, including the government, may save costs in management operations by using blockchain. Blockchain securely shortens transaction times and costs for money and information. Blockchain offers systems that automatically carry out agreed orders, parameterize signed contracts by requiring compliance, and provide transparent delivery methods. The future is wonderful.

WHY ARE BANKS (AND NON-BANKS) USING THIS TECHNOLOGY IN INCREASING NUMBERS?

Although blockchain is a relatively young technology, it is currently the finest data certifier and validator ever created. Additionally, as we already said, deploying dispersed data chains may improve process times and cut down on administration expenses.

How could companies and organizations not want this technology with that in mind?

Financial institutions represent a unique scenario. Their pre-Blockchain status is pretty unique.

On the one hand, people are compelled to comprehend and participate in the Blockchain game since anybody may set up a virtual bank in reality. Financial start-ups, or "fintechs," are developing financial ecosystems that are separate from the major banks, and when new laws like the PSD2 directive are implemented, this new rivalry is growing even more. All of this motivates them to advance.

On the other hand, they are subject to extremely strict restrictions, they have invested a lot of money in developing operating systems that really function, their customers are highly satisfied, and their average age is fairly high.

As a result of their conservatism and the fact that they are still some time away from an online industrial revolution, they are wary of a technology that they do not completely comprehend. So that's why they're being cautious there.

HOW COULD THIS TECHNOLOGY CHANGE INTERACTIONS BETWEEN PERSONS AND ORGANIZATIONS?

The next step with Blockchain will unquestionably influence two crucial qualities: reputation and veracity, in both personal and institutional connections.

Online fraud and deception will become more challenging as digital identification systems and data validation technologies progress.

The goal of the European Union is to advance the problem of distinctive digital identity registries so that our citizenship transcends the internet.

Blockchain in the workplace: 4 applications

The methods in which Blockchain might enhance current procedures and the ways in which this technology can open up new possibilities and business models are not always evident, however. With some specific examples of the most intriguing operational initiatives, we strive to illuminate the key ways that Blockchain and Distributed Ledger technology may provide value in the business environment in this article.

Over 1,242 announcements, trials, and operational projects using blockchain technology have been analyzed by the Blockchain & Distributed Ledger Observatory between 2016 and 2020. The Observatory examined 508 implementation projects from this study, identifying the key applications of Blockchain and Distributed Ledger technologies, and classifying them into four major groups based on the goals they seek to achieve: value exchange, data verifiability, data coordination, and the implementation of trustworthy processes.

1. Value trading

These are software programs that make use of the crypto-assets made possible by Blockchain platforms to trade money or other valuable assets in an unmediated and safe way. In 13% of the initiatives, the use of intermediaries is minimized or completely eliminated in order to streamline the flow of value between various participants.

JP Morgan's JPM Coin initiative is one such. By releasing its own digital version of the dollar (stablecoin), JPM Coin seeks to significantly eliminate inefficiencies in cross-border wholesale payments.

2. Reproducibility of data

Applications in this category make advantage of the immutability and transparency features of Blockchain technology by registering certain data or document attributes on it, making them visible and verifiable to other ecosystem members as well as to outside actors. In the survey, this category includes 24% of the initiatives. This group includes "notarization" applications, such as timestamping documents to confirm their creation date and to ensure they haven't been altered over time. In order to provide the end user more assurances about the traceability of goods, several initiatives of this kind have been established in the agri-food industry.

For instance, the IBM Food Trust project utilizes the Hyperledger platform to record the numerous processes that food items go through, increasing the transparency and dependability of the food supply chain.

3. Coordination of data

The majority of the examined use cases (59% of the projects) apply Blockchain and Distributed Ledger technologies to data sharing procedures. These technologies not only notarize information but also use smart contracts to enable on-chain data exchange, facilitating more effective and efficient coordination between various actors.

These apps are generally created to make it possible to reconcile information held by several participants, preventing the onset of misunderstandings and conflicts. Blockchain often takes the place of middlemen in these ventures.

One example is the platform created by Komgo to automate and expedite trade finance operations, which is built on the Quorum platform (a private version of Ethereum), enabling businesses to seamlessly exchange data and accompanying documentation.

Another example is the solution that Coca-Cola is promoting, which uses the Baseline protocol to link corporate ERPs, Hyperledger Fabric, and the Ethereum public blockchain to improve supply chain coordination and enable suppliers to access outside assistance in difficult situations.

4. The use of dependable procedures

The most ambitious initiatives come under this category, aiming to run whole company processes on Blockchain to make sure every step is verifiable. These initiatives use smart contracts on a Blockchain platform to encrypt the business process. Clearly, it is also the most difficult application scenario to achieve; in fact, just 4% of the projects examined to far meet this objective.

Despite this, it is already feasible to see this use case in certain real-world initiatives. For instance, Santander controlled the full bond issuance process on Ethereum in 2019 by handling both the on-chain and via stable crypto-assets the payments of the bond's interest.

What is necessary for the creation of business applications?

However, there are key components that still need to be completely developed in order to fully use the potential of these technologies and provide creative applications:

The ecosystems supporting Blockchain initiatives must be flexible enough to accept new users into a program;

Platforms that are both permissionless and permissioned must provide consistent performance in terms of scalability and security.

- The layer 2 solutions (such as the Lightning Network and rollups) and protocols like Baseline on Ethereum or the upcoming Taproot upgrade on Bitcoin, which also aims to increase privacy in these platforms, are some examples of how Permissionless are continuing their development path to overcome these limitations.

- Applications must be able to integrate with the information systems that companies are currently using; Applications must be able to rely on a regulatory framework that defines clear rules but leaves open the possibility of innovation; Applications must be able to leverage specific enabling services, such as s, in the permissioned ones instead, the performance improvement is strongly contributing to the evolution of protocols, such as Corda or the different versions of Hyperledger;

Cash on chain as a facilitating element

The latter issue is one of the most important and contentious, particularly in light of how the Central Bank Digital Currency (CBDC) phenomena has developed. Cash on chain, or the ability to use a fiat currency's digital equivalent directly within a blockchain platform, may make it possible to move some business operations entirely to the technology and pave the way for the development of truly novel applications that fall under the category of "reliable processes" implementation projects.

More than 24% of central banks are reportedly engaged in these initiatives, and some are either fully operational—as in Cambodia or the Bahamas—or in the experimental stages—as in China or Sweden. The European Central Bank, on the other hand, made its work on the Digital Euro public in October and will consider Distributed Ledger technology as one of the implementation options in 2021.

The method of investing in cryptocurrencies is considerably different from purchasing equities, despite the fact that it may first seem to be comparable. Instead of purchasing shares when you invest in a cryptocurrency, you purchase digital tokens from a third party in return for either a fiat currency or your own digital tokens. To make things more complicated, different cryptocurrency types serve different transactional functions, and even those that don't function as currencies in the conventional sense are nonetheless purchased for purely speculative reasons.

A very tiny percentage of people are really now utilizing cryptocurrencies in any significant manner, despite the fact that the volume of discourse around the issue could make it appear like everyone is investing in one form or another. This implies that you still have a chance to join the bitcoin industry as a whole from the beginning. There are certainly those out there whose price per unit has already exceeded $1,000 or even $10,000, but they are the exception, not the norm.

This use rate depicts an extremely positive future for bitcoin when taken in the context of its market capitalization and present level of hype. As a result, even if cryptocurrency as a whole continues to experience high levels of volatility, this volatility is expected to decrease significantly in the future. Until the moment of widespread saturation, that is, of course. The price bubble that has permeated the industry since its beginning will finally explode when more individuals use cryptocurrencies than do not.

When this happens, it is quite probable that the great majority of cryptocurrencies now available on the market will collapse in a manner reminiscent to the dotcom disaster of the late 1990s. This is why it's crucial to choose a cryptocurrency that has a verifiable worth rather than one that is based only on speculation, since the latter is far more likely to survive the impending collapse.

Select a cryptocurrency and an exchange: Prior to moving on, you should choose a cryptocurrency that makes sense for you. To achieve this, you should first carefully weigh the advantages and disadvantages of each cryptocurrency. The best option is something that will maximize your investment potential while remaining within your budget. Buying one ether is probably not the greatest use of your money if you just have $1,000 to invest but still want to strike while the iron is hot. It might be better to begin with perhaps 500 units of Lumens or 1,500 units of Ripple, two lesser-known cryptocurrencies targeted at developing nations that rose from $0.02 to $.62 per unit between October and December 2017.

In the preceding illustration, ether, ripple, and lumens each have a strong real-world use that adds value above and beyond what traders presently estimate their value to be. On the Ethereum platform, ether is used to power apps and transactions using smart contracts. Lumens are primarily aimed at a segment of the market that has, up until this point, had limited access to standard banking services that the majority of the globe takes for granted. Ripple is used to enable business-to-business transactions. The key to your long-term investment success is picking a cryptocurrency that has a clear purpose for being. Keep in mind that the more beneficial, the better.

Once you have one or two cryptocurrencies in mind, you should think about the numerous exchanges that provide the cryptocurrencies you are interested in. Your alternatives may significantly change depending on your decision, so if you do have a choice, it's critical to conduct your homework and make sure the exchange is fair and charges acceptable costs. You should look for an exchange that provides transaction charges based on a percentage of the entire transaction amount if you want to make several smaller transactions. You should look for an exchange that provides flat fees if you want to make fewer, bigger transactions.

After selecting an exchange, you must verify your account, which often takes a few days and requires different tiers of personal data to guarantee you have full access to your account. But if you currently own a cryptocurrency of some kind, you may often begin utilizing a new exchange with almost any verification needed.

No matter how great your first investment may appear on the surface, it is a smart idea to diversify after you have gained some experience with a particular cryptocurrency. Instead of doubling down on what could ultimately turn out to be too much of a "good" thing, it is nearly always going to be more practical to divide your entire investment cash into at least two areas. When this happens, building a portfolio will be necessary. If one is serious about investing, they should take this into account since it is an essential component of investing over the long run.

Additionally, diversifying will make it simpler to safeguard the gains you do earn from your investments, which should be your first priority given the extreme amount of volatility that all cryptocurrencies often experience. Your risk tolerance, your level of general investing comfort, and how much time you are ready to devote to micromanaging your assets will all have an impact on how you finally decide to allocate your funds.

In order to guarantee that you have a broad understanding of the types of patterns it moves in on a regular basis, it is also vital to look at the historical price data that is accessible when investing in cryptocurrencies. Understanding the internal workings of the cryptocurrency you chose will help you make the best judgments when the price decreases quickly. Each cryptocurrency has its unique internal workings. This kind of decline may be sometimes anticipated if you want to invest for the long term, and it will generally not cause you any concern. However, sometimes it can just be the beginning of a much steeper slide, and you need to be ready to recognize that since no investment is ever always the best option.

ICOs

The initial coin offering, or ICO, is a different way to invest in cryptocurrencies that is now gaining popularity. In reality, more than a billion dollars were generated in this way in 2017, with prominent leaders Bancor and Status.im raising $150 million and $75 million, respectively, on their first day of trading.

Initial coin offers are a play on the idea of an initial public offering, but other than the name, they have nothing in common with their namesake. ICOs are really just a new method for blockchain and cryptocurrency startups to crowdfund their innovative ideas. To do this, an early round of the cryptocurrency that will (theoretically) form the foundation of this new venture is released at a price that is (theoretically) far lower than what it will be worth when things are up and running.

If everything goes according to plan, investors get in early and the firm in question receives the funding necessary to complete the first development of their product or service in return for the potential for quick profits. Even though it is fundamentally riskier than investing in other sorts of known cryptocurrencies, the particular coin simply has to see one particularly significant upsurge for it to ultimately turn out to be successful. However, this is far from a certainty. The Ethereum platform has so far served as the foundation for the bulk of activity in the ICO market.

Investors from all over the globe have been known to open their wallets if the price is right, despite the fact that China, which has a history of demonstrating a strong commitment to the progress of blockchain and cryptocurrency technologies, provided the majority of the early ICO investment. However, before you do so, it's crucial to remember that investing in an ICO naturally has a number of other limitations as well.

The Securities and Exchange Commission has previously looked into various initial coin offerings (ICOs) in order to determine if laws, such as approval of company basics and a viable business strategy, were being circumvented. The little regulation that exists in this industry is already being circumvented, despite the fact that they are not held to the same criteria as an IPO. Many observers also point out that the first boom in this market is probably simply another manifestation of the kind of price bubble that has dogged cryptocurrencies since they were first introduced.

Nevertheless, this does not imply that the correct ICO lacks investment potential, since ICOs may undoubtedly provide sizeable profits for those willing to look beyond their added risk. When it comes to that risk, it's vital to bear in mind that the typical cryptocurrency is almost 10 times as volatile as the typical stock on the S&P 500 and around five times more volatile than gold. Because of this, investing in any of the less well-known cryptocurrencies puts you at a risk level that no institutional investor would ever think about. If you want to be successful in the long run with an ICO, you must thoroughly comprehend what you are entering into and be dedicated to the concept.

Approach each and every ICO with a critical eye to make sure you are choosing the most financially responsible course of action. This implies that you should begin by carefully examining all of the information that is readily accessible to you on the firm in issue.

This implies that you should make sure the business plan you are given can demonstrate a market need for the product or service the firm will be providing, and that the numbers add up over the long term. Additionally, it is crucial to make sure that the cryptocurrency in question fits into the company's overall strategy rather than seeming like an afterthought.

Additionally, it's critical to remember that investing in an ICO in no way entitles you to the advantages often connected with an IPO. As a result, you won't acquire any business shares, which also means you won't have any influence over the firm's future actions. Without anything physical like shares, you also miss out on the rules and commitments that govern IPOs, such as the accreditation and fiduciary duties. You only get a single deal on a new cryptocurrency, so it has to be a very great bargain for you to take on that much more risk.

Additionally, while working with an ICO, you should anticipate having access to the finished product or, in many cases, even a prototype. In fact, if you can produce a whitepaper, website, and business strategy all at once, you may think of your ICO as especially on the money. It is crucial now more than ever to never spend more in this kind of project than you can afford to lose since you typically won't have much to go on.

Furthermore, it's crucial to avoid letting any of the excitement that was around the firm at the time of the ICO affect your choice. After all, there is no assurance that this degree of customer knowledge and goodwill will last until the product is really released into the wild, particularly if that release is years away. All things considered, it may be wiser to spend your money elsewhere for the time being, at least until the first batch of ICOs is released and it is known if any of these early investments will provide a substantial return.

Using Ethereum for programming

Ethereum is a great platform for smart contracts since they operate on a prominent level that will keep the space in the bytecode of the virtual machine before letting it travel to the blockchain so that it may be performed. The majority of contracts are written by solidity, as you saw in the last chapter, but some will also be written using LLL, mutant, and serpent. Due to the fact that Python and JavaScript are two of the most widely used programming languages, you will discover that they are included in every programming language you use with Ethereum.

A new language named Viper has been developed for ethereum as a result of research. Viper will be a descendant of Python, but it won't function outside of ethereum. This implies that you must use Python in place of Viper if you wish to build other types of programs. Any type of Python will be acceptable.

The public will be able to see contracts that have been saved on the Ethereum blockchain. However, because the nodes will be attempting to compute the contract in real time, one of the drawbacks of Ethereum is that it will have performance concerns when it comes to the nodes, which will result in slower performance speeds.

Although sharding computations have been the focus of Ethereum programmers' attention, no answer has yet been discovered. A new protocol was implemented in 2016 to enable twenty-five transactions per second. Later that year, Ethereum's founder said that in order to make Ethereum more effective for its users, its scalability needed to be increased.

To make the blockchain platform tamper-proof, a number of different procedures will be implemented.

Issues with Ethereum You May Experience

Whatever it is, there will always be factors that will halt progress when something is new. These issues will make it more difficult for users to manage the platform and its applications. However, if you are aware of what is preventing you, you may work around it and continue to utilize the system as if these problems don't exist.

The scalability of Ethereum will be the first obstacle you encounter. The Ethereum network will only be able to handle seven transactions per second, contrary to the claims made about the operation of conventional payment networks, which are often repeated. However, you will have the option to modify the limit settings so that more transactions may be completed in a second. There's always a chance Ethereum may become too large and need consumers to operate complete nodes. However, some firms will be the only ones able to pay the resources required to operate that node if a whole node is demoted. As a result, certain Ethereum operations do not need you to download the blockchain.

The architecture of the blockchain, which will aid in maintaining the security that Ethereum provides in order to guarantee the maximum size of the most powerful nodes that will operate in supporting the large volume of transactions that are being processed, will thus be the biggest issue.

Additional factors that may result in scalability concerns include:

the number of users on the network.

users of either specialized or non-specialist gear. A specialized piece of equipment will have greater power than an unspecialized one.

the likelihood that unspecialized hardware will be used by the majority of users.

In order to reverse certain transactions, blocks will need to have 51 percent of the network's hash power available. However, the answer is for transactions to pay modest fees in exchange for a reduced degree of protection. This will require users to stay away from circumstances in which a network attacker may carry out an attack on a select few transactions in an attempt to benefit from their activities.

The majority of circumstances will try to maintain the characteristics that will help spread the account's blockchain. The solutions, however, will be unique to the domain registrations, digital money, or other peculiar situations that are appropriate.

With Ethereum, time stamping will also be a problem. A block will typically be formed every 10 minutes. But if a block is made every day, the system will be too sluggish, and if blocks are produced too quickly, the platform would get overloaded and have performance problems. Because of this, there is a "happy medium" that allows the blocks to be formed promptly without negatively impacting the system's performance.

Therefore, a distribution creation challenge involving the incentive-compatible system will be the main concern. To precisely maintain the time, this calls for an overlay to be placed on top of the block or chain.

Additional time stamping issues include:

Any user that uses a clock to create standard distributions for what is thought of as real-time will be off by 20 seconds.

The fact that a message originates from one node and is received by another node at a distance of never less than twenty seconds between the two nodes.

There may be solutions that depend on the nodes already in place. However, in order to be implemented, this procedure will need proof of stake or a non-Sybil token.

Some users have proposed that the system should provide a time that is at least 120 seconds behind the machine's internal clock. Nearly 99% of the participating nodes will be affected by this, forcing them to do the necessary actions. Note that this necessitates the system being self-consistent in less than 109 seconds.

The system will thereafter be able to function without users having to provide verification of their contributions.

The newly established system will be used by the external system. This implies that regardless of the motivation, it will continue to be safe against an attacker that wants to control 25% of the nodes.

There are additional issues that might prevent you from utilizing the Ethereum platform smoothly. The system's creators are making a lot of effort to remove obstacles and improve usability. But it won't make the issue go away immediately. The system itself may sometimes have issues, and the developers may not always be able to resolve them.

Users will inevitably discover issues that developers overlook. Therefore, you must report any difficulties you uncover so that they may be added to the list of problems that the developers are aware of and must address. By reporting issues, you can improve the system for everyone who uses it, including other users.

As you are aware, developers work to address issues that are reported by users, thus any issues that are discovered must be reported. You must bear in mind that the developers are also people, and they will have their own lives to manage in addition to their work. The Ethereum platform is built from a lot of code, which means there is a lot of code to look through in order to properly solve every problem. There will inevitably be problems that develop and persist for a time. Have trust in the developers since they will solve the issues that have been raised, and you'll see that the platform will function more effectively as a result of people like you!

www.ingramcontent.com/pod-product-compliance
Lightning Source LLC
Chambersburg PA
CBHW050247120526
44590CB00016B/2256